REPUTATION TO REWARD

Mastering Your Brand *Signature* to Earn More, Lead More, Win More

Yolanda Smith

Reputation to Reward: Mastering Your Brand
Signature to Earn More, Lead More, Win More

Copyright © 2019 by Yolanda M. Smith

Library of Congress Cataloging-In-Publication Data

Smith, Yolanda M.

ISBN 978-1-5136-6069-1

1. Women & Business   2. Image & Etiquette

Library of Congress Control Number:

Cover design by Stacey Grainger

Interior design by Stacey Grainer

Printed in the United States of America

First Edition

CONTENTS

FOREWORD

John Maxwell, leadership guru, says it best, "Everyone Communicates, Few Connect". There is an exchange that takes place in communication. What you say, how you say it, and how you show up curates an imprint of who you are to the receiver. Messaging then, becomes an impression. What you repeatedly impress upon others translates into branding, and branding is your business character on the world stage.

When some people think of branding, they are confused as to what it is. Branding is more than a look. It is a feel, a way of being. This is critical in clarifying what you want and who you want to serve. Get this right, and you attract the right clients—those who vibe with you on a deeper, rather than superficial level.

Yolanda brilliantly asks the right questions, so clients reveal the right representation and reputation that aligns to their highest intentions. In the business world, this level of intimacy, or connection, goes beyond the glitz. This distinguishes you from the crowd in an increasingly competitive market. Yet, not everyone makes the link between the exposure of their highest values and business character. More often, character ties to a personality rather than the soul of business.

The ability to communicate your values is directly related to success. This involves a continuous process of developing and maintaining a reputation that influences perception. In order to position yourself as the "go-to" expert in your field and connect with your ideal client's, you need more than a color scheme, fancy business card, crafty logo, or clever slogan—you need credible messaging that consistently speaks to your principles. That's a golden connection!

Warren Buffet, American business magnate and philanthropist, said he could lose billions overnight and earn it back, but his reputation was something different. The essence of Buffet's presentation during a shareholder's meeting, conveyed the idea that one's reputation must be crafted with care and guarded even more consciously. He shared "We can afford to lose money—even a lot of money. But we can't afford to lose reputation—even a shred of reputation."

What Yolanda does so well, is support her clients in identifying key values that demonstrate how to walk their talk with clarity, confidence, and conviction. This book is the competitive advantage that offers a blueprint to standing up and out among a crowded platform.

Consider this a personal invitation to walk alongside Yolanda as she takes you by the hand and shows you how to move from a business card to a business character.

Here's to a powerful and connected brand,

Linda Clemons
Sales & Body Language Expert

DEDICATION PAGE

This book is dedicated to my mom Loretta P. Whitlock, my LoLo whose unconditional love and support inspires me to always do my best, be kind, laugh often and take nothing for granted. She has such a giving heart, a selfless spirit and has served others throughout her life. Mom instilled in me that I can do anything I set my mind to, and that no mountain is too high to climb. I believed her and hung onto every word. She also instilled that these things could only be accomplished if I worked hard, and said on many occasions, you will have to work twice as hard as many of your counterparts. Mom was a hard worker and she taught us the importance of a good work ethic and perseverance. She has been a great role model and example for our family.

My mother is a beautiful, spiritual woman with a smile that can light up the room. She could turn a dollar into twenty and was rarely without an opinion. Her life experiences were unmatched to any degree you could obtain from the university. She had a street degree, she did not learn by reading, she learned through living, and in my opinion, that is a true PhD. Growing up as a kid whose mother passed away at a very young age, she faced may challenges. At times, life was very difficult. She was faced with a lot of "ism's": racism, colorism, classism, criticism, sexism and who knows what other ism's, yet she persevered, always putting one foot in front of the other, and trusting God to lead her path. She didn't have an appetite for excuses.

At the time of this writing, my LoLo is battling small cell lung cancer. I see daily her determination to keep fighting, never giving up. Through the pain and suffering, her will is strong and she's still feisty at times. She manages to find the good in all things, giving the praise and glory to God, despite what she has been through and is going through. It is a privilege to care for her and my prayer is that she does not leave this earth without knowing, beyond a shadow of doubt, how much she is loved and admired, how much we truly appreciated her sacrifices and dedication and how we remain in awe of her strength and courage.

Thank you for being my mom. I love you LoLo!

PREFACE

As I reflect on my life, I realize that I have learned some very valuable lessons. As a little girl, I had something special—the "it," the thing that people called sassy, feisty, mischievous, a go-getter. I am not sure exactly what you call it, but I had it. I was personable, well-liked and had an intellectual curiosity. I knew early on that I wanted a good life. I craved more than what was in front of me. You see, there are things that you cannot control. You cannot control who your family is, and I thank God I was fortunate to have a great family. My parents and my siblings were great. I love them dearly, and to this day, we are all still very close. At an early age, you cannot control your surroundings, your environment, or your circumstances, be they social determinants, economic advantages or disadvantages, or otherwise.

What I understood is that you can control how you react, that you can control your attitude, your behavior, and your destiny. As I look back, I realize that I was keenly aware of my surroundings. Television gave me a different perspective on life, and I liked it: there was a whole big world out there. My mom instilled confidence in me, and I believed her. My imagination allowed me to dream, and I welcomed it. I truly knew from an early age that I would not remain in my current environment. I engaged in things that were not natural for my environment (for example, waterskiing, snorkeling, and horseback riding). I actually owned a horse, Chachi, when I was 25. I wasn't scared to take risks. The world seemed like a big playground, and I wanted to play. Once I got my first job after college, I moved away from my hometown. It was time to explore.

You could say that I grew up in the hood, that would be slang for urban neighborhood. It's ok, and I am proud of my beginnings. The hood—the streets, if you will—is the best place to get your degree in life. This is where you separate the men and women from the boys and girls. You grew up fast, and either you made it out or you didn't. Ultimately, the choice was yours if you had the presence of mind to believe it.

I was mature beyond my years. I liked hanging with the older kids. I felt empowered, accepted, and grown-up. I paid attention, I absorbed knowledge, and I was fortunate enough to discern good from bad. That doesn't mean I didn't make mistakes or wrong choices from time to time, but it meant that I knew how to take the good out of the situation and work it to my advantage. I had the gift of gab and I was comfortable learning from others. I was a good student, not only in school but also in the streets. I was gifted with common sense as well as book sense, so I did ok for myself growing up.

I chuckle as I think about my consciousness as a youngster. I was aware of my appearance, and I believed that it mattered because people judge you. I was very stylish (my mom saw to that). I always dressed nicely and followed the latest trends. I was aware of how I presented myself, I was articulate, and most of the time I wanted to put my best foot forward to make a good impression. I was aware of how others perceived me, and when I received positive attention, I liked it and quickly learned the behaviors I needed to exhibit to gain positive affirmations.

I was unconsciously branding myself and creating an impression in the minds of others. I often was picked to speak in class or chosen to lead in some way. I was popular as I entered junior high and high school because I knew how to connect with people and build relationships. I possessed the likability factor, and to me, that was important. In hindsight, my actions were very intentional. I had some juice as the youngsters say—today, we call it influence. Branding has always been in my blood, and it's no wonder that I pursued a career in sales and marketing; it was a natural fit.

However, while I had some innate instincts around personal branding, I certainly did not know that is what it was called. As I started my professional career, I found out that there was so much I simply did not know. What I did know was that I was hungry—hungry to make a mark and to achieve success, to have financial freedom in my life, and to see the world beyond my hometown in Indiana. Yes, I am a Hoosier and proud of it. Indiana has a homegrown feel with a city appeal.

My hunger would often get me in trouble because I did not know how to channel my energy. I was not polished and did not have mentors and coaches to guide me. This was a huge gap in my development. Learning these things later in life brought back a hunger, yet it is a different type of hunger. Today my hunger and passion are to share the knowledge I wish I'd had in the earlier days of my career.

INTRODUCTION

"Reputation to Reward" will not only take you on my journey, but it will also provide you with an opportunity to learn how to build and sustain a positive brand *signature* to earn more, lead more, and win more. Each chapter will provide information that you can use to expand your knowledge, including what a personal brand is, the importance of having a personal brand, what it means to live your life authentically, and a step-by-step system for creating and mastering your brand *signature*. You will learn how to tell your story and gain an understanding of the most common pitfalls and mistakes of personal branding. Because you chose my expertise to guide you through your brand journey, I am providing bonus content to help you maximize your social media presence to create a positive digital footprint along with important information on managing your personal brand *signature* through a crisis.

When I first started writing the book, I was going to title it "Unleashing the Power of Personal Branding to Achieve Joy and Success." I just loved that title. I know it is my mission to help clients unleash the power of personal branding, but it was probably not going to attract readers. The title was too long, a bit on the soft side, and too intangible. People want some meat on their bones, they need to know what the outcome will be, so I had to go back to the drawing board. I ran through pages and pages of potential titles, and nothing was hitting me the right way. I never in a million years would have thought titling a book would be this hard.

Then, after brainstorming with one of my coaches, I came up with "Converting Reputation to Revenue." Initially, I loved this title. I was like, "Yeah, baby! I got this!" I shared it with my friends, and several liked the title or at least the concept, yet others struggled with the revenue part. Additionally, several people shared with me that "Reputation to Revenue" did not resonate with my brand. However, after settling down the excitement I was feeling, I understood that not everyone is motivated by money, that it is not the be-all end-all to an individual and what a powerful brand *signature* can offer. But I still liked it. It rolled off the tongue, had a nice ring to it, if you will, but deep inside I knew it was not the one.

On a brisk January morning, around three o'clock a.m., I was suddenly awakened. My eyes popped open, and it hit me: "Reputation to Reward." That was it! I instantly knew that was the title for my book. Reward can mean what the reader wants it to mean and can be as tangible of an outcome as you choose it to be. For some, it may be career advancement, accumulating wealth, promotion and recognition, or building power and influence. For others, it may be living authentically, developing meaningful relationships, deepening your spirituality, creating power networks, gaining social media followers, operating in your passion, attracting clients, and the list goes on and on. Whatever the reward, I love the idea that YOU, as the CEO of your brand, can define it. I view this as a huge responsibility, one not to be taken lightly, that puts you in the driver seat.

You are officially in control of your brand. I believe in you and know that you are reading this book because you want to develop a personal brand that can yield rewards. Countless others have succeeded by having a strong brand *signature*, and for every one of those, there are three times as many who have failed. Failure does not come from trying, it comes from not knowing, not believing—yes, that is correct, not knowing that having a powerful personal brand is a requirement in today's world.

I, as your personal "Brandthrupist," the person who will guide you on your personal brand journey to master your brand *signature*, will be with you every step of the way. Shall we get started? Time waits for no one.

> "It must be borne in mind that the tragedy of life doesn't lie in not reaching your goal. The tragedy lies in having no goal to reach.
>
> It isn't a calamity to die with dreams unfulfilled, but it is a calamity not to dream.
>
> It is not a disaster to be unable to capture your ideal, but it is a disaster to have no ideal to capture.
>
> It is not a disgrace not to reach the stars, but it is a disgrace to have no stars to reach for.
>
> Not failure, but low aim, is sin."

BENJAMIN MAYS

Chapter 1

What is Personal Branding?

The song "Who Are You? Who, Who… Who, Who ♫ ♫" performed by the rock group, The Who, is stuck in my head as a grim reminder that I blew a huge opportunity to articulate my value to the most senior person in my organization. It was a spring afternoon in 2009, and I was in a spacious conference room with a diverse group of creative colleagues working on an employee engagement project when the CEO of our company entered the room.

He began introducing himself to each of us, and it was obvious he knew some of the individuals in our group, but when he came to me and I introduced myself, he said, "Hello Yolanda, I don't believe we've ever met." I acknowledged that, and he said, "Tell me, what do you do?" I froze, and with my heart racing, I timidly stuttered my job title. I recall saying, "I'm just a…" but before I could get it out, I nervously giggled. He looked amused and immediately moved to the next person. Instantly, I knew I had not made a great impression, nor would I be memorable. I also knew that I could never take back that moment.

That experience stayed with me for years, and I often replayed that event in my mind, trying to figure out what I could have done differently. Nonetheless, time passed, and I eventually moved on to other roles. I will say that, over the years, that CEO and I crossed paths on multiple occasions, and on each encounter, it was like he was meeting me for the first time. It appeared that he had no recollection of having met me, and I, still haunted by that day, never attempted to help him recall that initial meeting. I was simply hoping he did not ask the dreaded question, "What do you do?"

At that point, I had held several sales and marketing positions with a few companies, and I would characterize my career as relatively successful with the usual ups and downs. However, because of that dreadful encounter with that CEO in 2009, I was no longer sure of who I was. Why couldn't I put it into words? Why was I afraid to be my authentic, sassy self and tell him like I have told countless others that "I lead transformation initiatives with confidence, innovation, and agility to innovate, deliver results, and challenge the status quo"? After all, I had led the effort to enter the company into the social media space and had launched several award-winning health education platforms. Yet, somehow the words eluded me on that day, and the only thing that escaped my lips was my job title.

Now, looking back, I know what the problem was: you see, I had no personal brand. I did not have a story. I was moving mindlessly through my career without true intention and clarity of my professional identity, but that was about to change!

Creating Your Personal Brand

Everyone needs a personal brand—I mean an intentional and strategic brand *signature*, not one that is organically created. Personal branding is an ongoing process of developing and maintaining a reputation and impression. Your brand is your value, your promise to others. Your personal brand allows you to create the image you want others to see and obtain the rewards you desire. It is how you will be remembered, the way you communicate and interact with others, and it allows you to articulate your value and what differentiates you from others in the eyes of your audience.

Your brand *signature*, like your passion, will keep you standing when people try to knock you down. It establishes an impression and influences how others perceive you and connect with you. Your personal brand is how you communicate and demonstrate your relevance and business character. It is not only based on your competency but

> " **Your personal brand is how you communicate and demonstrate your relevance and business character.** "

also on your actions. Personal branding is what others say about you when you leave a room—when they are gossiping, are they speaking positively or negatively about you?

Personal branding used to be considered nothing more than a business card with your name and title on it. Nowadays, in order to stand out and build meaningful and intimate relationships with the people you want to serve, you need more than a brand color and logo to be successful. Owing to the growth of social media, today, the brand you build around yourself is perhaps the single most important thing that makes you stand out. We live in a world where your online reputation can be your strongest asset or your biggest liability. A world where sales and marketing are better executed by employees with strong personal brands than by the brands themselves. Where companies hire not based on resumes and cover letters, but on information they find online.

Take LinkedIn as an example, if you have a profile, chances are that you have been contacted by recruiters or organizations. I know that I am consistently being contacted by recruiters, organizations and individuals that want to connect and offer their goods and services. It is easier than ever to grow a vast following and become the go-to expert in your industry or field.

Personal branding is how you present yourself online and offline to people personally and professionally. It is how you define yourself and shape the way others see you. It is how you show up consistently.

Put simply, personal branding is the intersection between perception and reality.

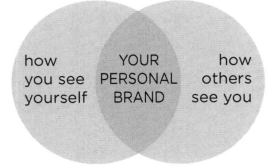

Personal branding is becoming less of a competitive edge and more of a requirement for anyone looking to grow their business; get that dream job; or take their career to the next level. Because it is a requirement in today's digital age; if you are not owning your personal brand and framing your story, someone else is doing it for you. It must be led by your voice and failing to manage your personal brand can cause misinformation to spread about you or your company. And that is risky because what others project onto you may not be how you wish to be perceived.

Let's examine the importance of this concept. Say, for example, that you are ambitious, innovative, and direct, but you have not created and managed a personal brand identity that articulates your value and shares your Why. Someone else may perceive your positive traits as negative and refer to you as pushy, aggressive, and brash. If that person starts to create that narrative about you and people do not know you or your story, perceptions can easily go sideways because the image you want people to see is in stark contrast to what is being said about you. You are the entrepreneur of your personal brand. Take ownership of it.

Steve Jobs is a great example of personal branding. His brand *signature* was very distinct, yet it became synonymous with Apple, and you knew what he and the Apple brand stood for. Think about it: it all started with a laptop, which was simpler and more convenient than a desktop. Apple's promise is to create products based on seeing the world a little differently, and they achieved this with miniaturization and functionality through

the iPhone, iPad, and Apple Watch. It was all about antici-
pating people's needs and delivering solutions with simplicity.
It is memorable, from Steve's attire of a black turtleneck and
jeans to the simple white Apple packaging that contains few
words. There was no mistaking him or the Apple brand. And
because the Apple brand is so well-defined, people stand in line
for hours to get the next product without truly knowing what
it will do but trusting that it will meet their needs. How crazy
is that? I buy something to meet a need that I don't know I
have. That is the epitome of a powerful, trusted brand. Yet,
what stands out for me is the deepening of relationships and
filling needs that matter not only in the here and now but also
in the future. Apple can anticipate what you need before you
know you need it. Now that's a powerful brand *signature* and is
Simply Brilliant!

1998   1999   2001   2004   2005   2007   2008   2009   2010

As you can see, an outstanding brand *signature* has many
advantages, including power and influence. Having influence
through recognition of your expertise and the power to make

6

things happen is very important in life. It allows you to get things done and make things happen. It can be game-changing, world-changing. You can literally cash in on your reputation—yes, you heard it from me, it can absolutely be monetized. From reputation to reward, a strong personal brand affords you many benefits that we will discuss in later chapters, but two of the greatest aside from influence and power are joy and success. Imagine living a life of joy and success. Joy is a feeling of great pleasure and happiness—now, who doesn't want or deserve that in their life? And success, well that one is a bit more ambiguous because success to one person is not success to another. You define what success means for you, so whether it is personal or professional, you can define and accomplish it. There is true power in your brand. You must believe it and claim it.

I would be remiss if I did not share with you what personal branding is not. Personal branding is not about showing off or selling yourself. It is not a logo or a tagline. It's not what you post on Facebook or respond to on Twitter. As a matter of fact, it is not about you at all; it's about the value you deliver to others.

I know, that's a hard pill to swallow, but let me explain. You can use your brand *signature* to market your value and gain influence and power, but ultimately, it's about making yourself available to others. It is what you provide others that, in turn, allows you the rewards of joy and success. I always share with my audiences that there are two types of people in the world.

- Those that use themselves to benefit others
- Those that use others to benefit themselves

Which one are you? Personal branding is about building your reputation, not self-promotion. Theodore Roosevelt said it best: "People don't care how much you know until they know how much you care."

Chapter Two

The Importance of a Positive Personal Brand

You may be asking yourself, "Why is personal branding important, and why should I care?" I am happy you asked those questions, but let me ask you a question: Would you like to increase your value, unlock your potential, live in your passion, have more money, overcome barriers, gain visibility, have more clients, or just get unstuck? Simply put, would you like to earn more, lead more, and win more while living a life of joy and success? A strong brand *signature* enables all those things.

Personal branding is important because it allows you the opportunity to share and embrace your authentic self while articulating your value to others. As I have shared, this is now a requirement for success and so often, people are unaware that personal branding exists. We spend time cultivating our organizations brand and helping them achieve the rewards of their identity, yet do not realize, we need the same for ourselves. If you have mentors or coaches and they have not mentioned the importance of creating an intentional and strong personal brand—your brand identity—I would be concerned. For me, it was certainly the case. I started college with no money and no idea that I could obtain financial aid because my mom, who was the breadwinner of our single-family household for much of my life, was a very hard-working woman, often working two jobs to care for my sibling and me, with little education or knowledge of the educational system. I graduated high school early, so I missed all the talk about college preparations and financial aid. Or perhaps they were there, and I just wasn't paying attention. I hope you caught that—you see, part of your personal brand is owning and accepting accountability.

This unfortunate misstep led me to my only option, at least in my mind: to pay for college with cash. So, I started an imprinted sportswear business, called Yotra Designs, with a friend to supplement my education and lifestyle while also working a full-time job. Seven years later, I graduated with a bachelor's degree, debt-free and ready to pursue my dreams, whatever that meant. I studied and majored in marketing and business analysis, and I wanted to be an interior designer or fashion designer though I couldn't draw a straight line. I had big dreams but no direction.

With no mentors, no coaches, and very little guidance, I lacked the knowledge and confidence that I needed to keep my business going even though it was profitable. Besides, I wanted a job that required that college degree that I had worked so hard to obtain. If I had known then what I know now, I would have remained an entrepreneur.

Life lessons like that allow us to grow, and as ambitious entrepreneurs and corporate professionals, we must learn to navigate the terrain. There will not always be someone there to hold your hand. With spunk and curiosity, I was determined to make my way, and I set out to find a "real job," ultimately landing a sales role in the pharmaceutical industry.

As I have often said and still believe to this day, if there was someone—a mentor, counselor, or coach—to guide me in my early career years, I could have gone further faster. It's easy to dwell on the what-ifs, yet I prefer to live in the here and now, and I don't look back unless there's a lesson to be learned.

I believe that being a curious learner and having a lot of initiative helped me in my career. I wanted to know about things, I asked a lot of questions, and I was sometimes inquisitive and bold to a fault. Some may call it nosey, but I prefer to jokingly call it having "high needs." I need to know. However, I recognize that my career and successes have been orchestrated purely by God's grace because I believe he looks out for babies and fools. Perhaps I also had a little dumb luck along the way if you believe in that.

And that brings me to the present day. I choose to operate in my passion and invest and instill knowledge, nuggets, and confidence in others so they will know what I certainly did not.

When you don't know what you don't know, you are disadvantaged when there are others who do. Yet, I also believe that when you know better, you should do better. My first formal mentor did not come until mid-career.

> **"When you don't know what you don't know, you are disadvantaged when there are others who do."**

While the expression "better late than never" rings true, my goal is to shout my knowledge from the mountaintops.

A personal brand is absolutely important, valuable, and necessary. I cannot say why I did not have knowledge of these things (personal branding, mentors, sponsors, etc.) earlier in my career, but what I do know is that it is common for women and minorities to be left in the dark. My mission is to shed some light to ensure you do not have to wait as long as I did to learn what I have learned. Don't be like me, be better equipped than me and master your personal brand *signature* to attain the rewards that your heart desires.

Today, job security is a discarded relic, pensions are going away, and gone are the days of individuals staying on one job for 15-20 years. The structures of organizations are becoming flatter, less siloed, and more cross-functional; being agile, flexible, and having recognition of your expertise allows you to unlock disruptive opportunities. Most people will change companies (or even careers) eight to ten times before retiring. We are living in a much different world today where the most important job you have is being the CEO of your own brand. We are all free agents, and success will be difficult unless people feel as though they know you. They need to feel like their experience with you is positive and genuine, and that feeling comes only with a personal connection and the ability to differentiate yourself from others.

The power and influence that emanates from a strong brand *signature* are immeasurable, as they take on many facets from personal to professional, spiritual to financial. When people believe they know you authentically, they get very enthusiastic. Life is about negotiations, and having a positive personal brand allows you to operate from a position of confidence and influence. When done with intention and purpose, the benefits of a personal brand far outweigh the risks.

Here are a few reasons to build a positive brand *signature*:

- Increase your value
- If you don't create your brand story, someone else will
- Enhance your recognition as an expert in your field
- Establish a reputation and credibility
- Build self-confidence
- Differentiate yourself from others
- Build networks, relationships, and more

As I continually research this fascinating topic, I come across great information from time to time. On one particular day, I stumbled upon an article in *Fast Company* called "The Brand Called You" by renowned author and speaker Tom Peters.

He stated, "it's a brand world" and continued by asking that if big companies understand the importance of brands, why shouldn't you? Regardless of age, regardless of position, regardless of the business we happen to be in, all of us need to understand the importance of branding. We are CEOs of our own companies: Me Inc. In today's business world, your singularly most important job is to be head marketer for the brand called You.

And I love his call to action. Tom said, "It's this simple: You are a brand. You are in charge of your brand. There is no single path to success. And there is no one right way to create the brand called You. Except this: Start today. Or else."

There you have it. Tom Peters said this in the late 1990s—fast forward to today, and his words are more critical than ever. You can evolve your brand, and the time is now. Companies are changing, trust is eroding, we are living in different times, and it comes down to two fundamental questions: "Why should someone pick you?" and "What makes you better suited than your competition?" You guessed it—a strong personal brand. Having a strong brand *signature* answers both those questions. It's about deepening relationships and building credibility to move from reputation to reward.

Chapter Three

What's in it for Me?

I realize it is human nature to want to understand the benefit of doing something before you do it. I get that, and it is absolutely the normal thing to ask. What's in it for me? When you are trying to understand the ROI of a project, product, or program, you certainly look for the benefits to outweigh the risk; you seek to understand the external environment; you are forecasting what type of outcome your investment will yield before making a decision. That's a natural part of the strategic process in determining the feasibility of moving forward and committing to invest resources.

Yet, have you ever been challenged by the statement: **It is not the benefit of doing something, instead it is the risk of not doing it**"? This is what I call the cost of doing business.

Ok, now stay with me, because this is important. Human nature has us always looking for the silver lining, the benefit, the result, but every now and then, we must say to ourselves, "What happens if I do nothing?" If you are in business, you are always analyzing different scenarios to understand the what-ifs by asking questions, and there are some questions that you should be asking but might not be. "What if I do nothing?" "What does that mean to me, my organization, and my business?" "What will my competition be doing?" "Will I become disadvantaged?" It is this same thought process that I want you to pressure test against your brand *signature*. Now, I do not want to scare you into thinking you must do it strictly for purposes of mitigating risk—there are great benefits and advantages to having a powerful personal brand.

The primary disadvantage of not having a personal brand is that you are not in control of your destiny. If you are allowing your personal brand to organically take on dimensions that sometimes yield positive results, your brand becomes a brand of chance instead of a brand of intention. The truth is that everyone is creating a personal brand. However, if you are not doing it strategically and intentionally, it's risky. You may be leaving your power on the table, and I am not talking about power in terms of a title, control over others, or a who's-climbing-over-who type of power.

If you want to control your brand, you must come to terms with your own power. I am talking about reputational power, influential power, the power that comes from being known for your contributions and expertise and reaping the rewards and benefits they afford you. For example, if you are a scholar or thought leader, it may be the number and types of publications you produce that are cited by others. If you are a consultant, it may be your expertise, power networks, and how many executive or email contacts you have. Think about it: our buying and association behaviors are attracted to brands because of the power

> **" Power is largely a matter of perception. "**

they project. Power is largely a matter of perception. If you desire to be a powerful brand, you must act like a credible leader, but not the leader of an organization—I am referring to you leading You. Again, you are the CEO of your brand.

When I began to learn about this, it really struck a chord with me, as I was in the throes of my career in corporate America. I had started growing my expertise and interest with intentionality and I quickly discovered a passion for educating and inspiring others. I took on roles where I could thrive in these areas, quickly becoming known for my innovative thinking and expertise in the areas of digital technology, relationship management, and personal branding. I started attending conferences and sharing my opinions, and before I knew it, I was being asked to speak and participate from a different position, a position of influence. It was exhilarating, and I enjoyed being revered as an expert, but more importantly, I gained the ultimate satisfaction from providing value to others. Still today, I get calls to speak on topics I no longer follow, but it is the influence and power of reputation that enables my name to be among those of experts.

I discovered my passion for personal branding when I took a seat on the board of directors of a non-profit girl's organization.

It was then that I realized there is more that must be done in addition to educating and inspiring others to achieve their best. I quickly learned that I needed to support others by providing the tools and practical steps to apply the teachings. My love for personal branding was born, my vision came into clear focus, and I have never looked back. I consider it an honor and privilege to share my expertise with individuals and organizations, early- and mid-career professionals, executives, and entrepreneurs from all backgrounds. We all need a personal brand. But it was only through the brand discovery process for myself, that I was able to figure out what I wanted to represent today and in the future.

Imagine this, WHAT IF—JUST WHAT IF—YOU SETTLED FOR MORE AND NOT LESS? What would that look like in your life? Would you like to be tapped on the shoulder for a promotion versus applying for the job? What if clients were seeking you out? Visualize the feeling of operating on all cylinders and being aligned personally, spiritually, and profes-sionally. What would that feel like? What if you had more than enough money, and your contact list and followers were plentiful? Could you handle living your best life, filled with personal accomplishments, financial freedom, family, friends and the ability to do what you choose?

Well, I can tell you, it is an amazing feeling, and you deserve and can have it all. You can program your mind to operate on a frequency that consistently empowers you to know it is possible. You can reject the limiting beliefs in your thoughts and operate with determination and confidence.

I know because I am a living testament to what a brand *signature* offers. I put my faith in God and know that whatever I ask shall be mine, if I am willing to put the work in. Several years back, someone asked me how I became successful, what is it that you did? Now, keep in mind, I was in sales at the time, and I stayed in the top sales rankings. Admittedly, one of my love languages is affirmations. I like a little public recognition every now and again. But my answer to this person was this: "I am successful because I believe I should be."

When I was young, my mom told me that I could be anything I wanted and that there was no one better than me. She repeated this throughout my childhood and guess what—I believed it. I could tell you stories about my time in small rural areas in the south, where I was the only black girl in town, calling on doctors to sell my products, being called "gal" and being told that I was taking away "the man's job" and his ability to care for his family, that I needed to be home in the kitchen... I refuse to go down this path because you can see where that was going.

But you know what? I didn't care. I made it my mission to win them over. I stayed true to myself, and in the end, they all eventually came around—well all except for one, but we won't talk about that. I was determined to build a relationship with all my customers, supporters and naysayers, and it was those relationships that ultimately gave me business and support for my products. It is no secret that this happened because people conduct business with people they like. I learned that lesson early. I am still evolving, yet it did not take long to see the rewards of my hard work. Yet you must be intentional, you must take action, and you must put forth the effort to help others see the value you can bring to them.

You are reading this book and I am grateful to have your trust and support. Believe it or not, one of the hardest things I do, still to this day, is to convince and influence individuals to take control of their own personal brand identity. Many do not believe this is important and it is by far, one of the most common personal branding mistakes one can make. No matter what your aspiration in life, how smart you are, or how much money you have, without a positive reputation and image, you may as well have nothing.

> "Regard your good name as the richest jewel you can possibly be possessed of."

SOCRATES

Having a strong brand *signature* benefits you in many ways, you can:

- Market yourself
- Advance your career
- Gain influence
- Position yourself for promotions
- Develop a powerful network

- Build relationships and trust
- Identify and leverage your competitive advantage
- Build authority and expertise
- Write a book, create a course, teach others
- Increase your visibility
- Celebrate your uniqueness and authenticity
- Live in your passion
- Attract others
- Stand out and prosper

From Reputation to Reward. I love that title because the reward is whatever you choose. You can reap the reward you desire with a strong brand *signature*. I use the word brand *signature* interchangeably with personal brand. The difference is that the term personal brand is broad and can be perceived as somewhat generic, while your brand *signature* is unique to you and only you! Yet no matter the term, a strong brand has its privileges.

Let's look at an example to illustrate how a strong personal brand can impact your income. On average, an individual with a strong personal brand earns 10-25% more annually than someone without a strong brand. For ease of computation, let's look at a case study of a business graduate.

CASE STUDY

- Starting salary: $52K a year
- Strong brand *signature* yields a 25% increase
- The net result is $65K a year

That's a pretty significant difference. And considering that 2/3 of lifetime wage growth occurs in the first ten years of a person's career, you can understand how this higher initial wage will be compounded over time.

Now, now, if you are beyond the 10-year career mark, don't fret: the point is that with a strong brand *signature*, you have more opportunities for increasing your wage, influence, promotion offers, bonus potential, ability to live your passion, etc. The impact and reward can be great whether you work for an organization or own your own business. Entrepreneurs have a higher stake in the game because their brand must be synonymous with their company's brand. Why, you ask? Because starting out in business, people will rely on your personal brand and story. They will need to trust you as the owner and believe in you until your business is established.

The great news is that using today's technology, anyone can create their own brand *signature*. One key to growing your brand and power is to recognize that we now live in a digital world and almost everything is done online. I won't lie and say it's easy, but everyone can stand out, and we all have a chance to learn, improve, and build our skills. No longer can you afford to be defined by your job title or job description. It takes dedication, consistency, and work, but it can, without a doubt, be accomplished.

You are brand-worthy.

Chapter Four

Looking in the Mirror

If no one has ever told you, allow me to be the first. You don't need to compromise to be recognized. I will share that again, you do not need to compromise to be recognized.

The beginning of my career as a sales representative became a pivotal moment for me. Fresh out of college, I set out to meet recruiters to help me find the ideal job. They unanimously concluded that I had the gift of gab and was a people person. I was presented to a major pharmaceutical company and interviewed for a sales position. I must tell you about that experience at some point because I wore a red dress to my original interview—which is a big no-no—but I had originally set out to sabotage the interview because I decided at the last minute that I did not want to relocate. God has a way of making it all work for your good, though. He gives us provision even when we cannot see the vision. I was offered the job and accepted.

Fresh out of sales training, I was excited to start calling on my physician customers. Armed with a portfolio of rehearsed sales pitches, detail aids, and canned answers to any question the doctor might pose, I was READY! I recall going into physicians' offices with my canned messages and getting strange reactions and very little alignment to what I was saying—clearly not quite what I expected. I was a bit disappointed. I would leave and think, "Hmm, they're the doctor. They should know more than me. This isn't rocket science, so why don't they seem excited?"

Yet, after a few weeks in the field, my district manager decided to come to my territory for a ride-along. We visited a few customers, and after the second call, he told me that we needed to talk. I wondered what I had done now. I bet you can tell from my writing; I can be a bit feisty and I don't shy away when it comes to sharing my opinion. He said, "Yolanda, I want you to put away the detail aids and simply hold a conversation with your customers."

Being new, as you can imagine, I wanted to do everything by the book, but that was not me. It didn't align with my communication style. It made me extremely uncomfortable, and it sounded terribly rehearsed. My personality and ability to connect were lost in translation when I tried to remember my script verbatim. My manager noticed, the customer noticed, I noticed, and it was during this discussion that he gave me a gift. My manager gave me permission to be my authentic self. From that moment, I was able to connect with customers, build long-lasting relationships, trust, and credibility. Over the next 15 years, I had a career I enjoyed and was very successful in.

When you are being yourself, you can perform at your best. I won numerous awards, trips, promotions and the respect of my customers and peers. Believe me, there is nothing like that feeling of being on top of the world, on top of your game for simply being YOU! Credit must also be given to that leader, if not for his recognition that I was not being myself, my career could have ended in failure. I became a selling machine.

What I learned is that when you are operating from a place of truth, authenticity, and genuineness, people relate to you, they understand and know your story, and therefore, they tend to be more inclusive. When people think they know who you are, they are more likely to support you, nominate you, promote you, sponsor you, marry you, and loan you money. Conversely, when you are not authentic, you can only keep that charade up for so long, and then a person's intuition will kick in, and they will detect your fakeness and question your legitimacy and realness. As a result, doors will unexpectedly be shut to you, or they might never open. And often times, people won't tell you how they feel, they just won't deal with you.

In our everyday lives, we are truly at our best when we can be our authentic selves. What does that mean? It means you are not being false or a copied version of someone else. You are being genuine and real, representing your true nature and beliefs. This is powerful. You wake up with the opportunity to be who you are and represent that to the world.

Be yourself—everyone else is already taken.

You are an original. Why be a copy?

I recognize that there are times when it is not that easy. I believe we live in a diverse world, where our uniqueness should be celebrated, where we should respect and accept differences of opinion, beliefs, ethnicities, and experiences, but unfortunately, that is not always the case. Companies and organizations establish history, and history sets a precedent for the culture they breed. Sometimes, that culture steeped in tradition does not allow for change, nor is it accepting of other's thoughts, ideas, and experiences, particularly if they are contrary to those of the company. As a result, we often see what is referred to as code-switching. What is that you say?

Code-switching is the practice of switching from one code to another either to show solidarity with a social group or organization, to distinguish oneself from others, to participate in social encounters, to discuss a certain topic, to express feelings and affections, or to impress and persuade an audience. In layman's terms, it's doing what is necessary to fit in, whether it means adjusting your language, behaviors, position, or perspective. It was first coined as cultural code-switching to account for linguistic and cultural behavioral differences, particularly when visiting foreign countries, but it has been popularized and is also known as behavior adopted in professional settings, and more commonly pinned to diverse populations who want to fit in and be successful.

While I will share with you that it is by far more rewarding to be authentic and true to yourself because when you are operating from a position of truth, you are more productive and can achieve greater joy and satisfaction. You must also recognize that it is important to assimilate and blend with other cultures to be successful. Doing so is what makes the world go round. It's about getting along to accomplish common goals. Diverse groups drive greater profits than any singular group, yet there is typically one group that has the controlling interest and sets the tone. So, ask yourself, "Have I been in situations where I put on a different persona or modified who I am to be successful and adapt in the workplace?" I guarantee that most of us would say yes, and not just the minorities—all of us. I am not saying it is a negative thing. However, if you are changing a large part of who you are and what you value to fit in and belong, perhaps you are associated with the wrong organization or group.

So, why are we talking about this? The reason is that we must hold ourselves as individuals, leaders and organizations accountable so that we can work in healthy, welcoming environments where our true thoughts, experiences, beliefs, and actions are encouraged, where we feel comfortable speaking up and challenging the status quo and bringing forth innovative ideas and solutions for better outcomes and

> **The truth is that people will respect you for being you.**

impacts. The truth is that people will respect you for being you. I love the quote by Bernard Baruch: "Those that mind don't matter, and those that matter don't mind."

Authenticity is a key requirement as you begin to cultivate your personal brand. You must know yourself—I mean really know yourself—in order to build a credible brand *signature*. As leaders, we must embrace the authenticity and inclusion of diverse populations and encourage individuals to bring their whole selves to work. Essentially, as an individual, you should feel comfortable and confident in who you are and allow others to see your talents and value.

Now, I am not saying that we should bring every behavior, action, belief, or attitude to work—you know, some things need to remain at home. The key is understanding your surroundings and knowing what is appropriate. If your work setting is very formal and conservative, coming in with facial piercings and rainbow hair may not be appropriate (keep in mind that every organization is creating and maintaining its own brand as well). You should be where your uniqueness is celebrated and valued. If you work for an organization, you must respect the image and reputation that the organization wishes to create, it is only fair.

However, what I am referring to is the ability to be yourself, speak up and be heard, share ideas and your cultural traditions and gender or identity experiences, wear your burka and hair natural and not be ridiculed, be respected for your beliefs (religious and otherwise), and so forth. Having a strong personal brand helps to build that platform; it is your opportunity to share and embrace your uniqueness while articulating your value.

I want you to pause for a moment to reflect on yourself, your uniqueness, the real you, and answer the following questions:

1. Who are you?

   _____

   _____

   _____

2. How do you show up?

   _____

   _____

   _____

3. How do you demonstrate self-awareness?

   _____

   _____

   _____

4. How do you put your authenticity to the test?

   _____

   _____

   _____

"Many people would be scared if they saw in the mirror, not their faces but their character."

UNKNOWN

Chapter Five

You Better Tell Your Story

As we begin to explore how building your brand *signature* can be accomplished, I am reminded of the time several years back when I started facilitating workshops on personal branding for young girls. After studying and researching, I found a common theme in delivering a presentation and personal branding. Essentially, when you give a presentation, you tell the audience what it is you are going to say, you say it, and then you remind them you said it. Personal branding is similar: you tell your audience what you are going to do—that is your promise and value to others; you show up and do it—you deliver what you promised—and then share with them that you did it. This becomes your story and because of the technology explosion social media can be your platform.

Before I explain the "how," I want you to take an inventory of your current personal brand. This is important because it gives you a baseline for where you are and helps define where you are going.

Start by identifying, then listing below the qualities or characteristics that make you distinctive from your competitors—or your colleagues.

You	Competitors/Colleagues
1.	4.
2.	5.
3.	6.

1. What have you done lately (this week) to make yourself stand out?

   _____

   _____

   _____

2. What would your colleagues or your customers say is your greatest and clearest strength?

   _____

   _____

   _____

3. What is your most noteworthy (as in, worthy of note) personal trait?

   _____

   _____

   _____

Then ask yourself these three questions.

1. What is your reputation?

   _____

   _____

   _____

2. How do others perceive you?

   _____

   _____

   _____

3. Does your personal identity match your public reputation?

   _____

   _____

   _____

Now, let's put your brand to the test. Write down six words or more that describe you, and don't share them with anyone.

1.	4.
2.	5.
3.	6.

Ask your friends, family, and colleagues what their experience or relationship with you is like. Ask them to describe you as a friend, family member, and co-worker. Have them list at least six words that describe you. Now, populate the charts and compare their words to yours.

Family	
1.	4.
2.	5.
3.	6.

Friends	
1.	4.
2.	5.
3.	6.

Colleagues	
1.	4.
2.	5.
3.	6.

Are the answers the same or similar in meaning? Are the answers what you expected? If they are the same or similar, you are doing a great job of creating your personal brand. If they are not, you, my friend, have some work to do. It's ok— that's why you're reading this book.

When I did this exercise, I was surprised to see how the descriptive words from others of me were, at points in time, all over the place. We know we show up differently at work than at home, differently with our friend's than our coworkers, etc. However, what we are striving to achieve is synergy and alignment between all groups because if we are similar across groups (friends, co-workers, family), that indicates that we are living authentically and do not have to change who we are depending on the company we keep. Now, as I shared in the "Living Authentically" chapter, not every behavior or action at home needs to be mirrored at work, but again, we want similarities.

When I asked my then-12-year-old to describe me, she said I was anal, alive, intentional, intelligent, important, authentic, and fabulous. I was certainly in agreement that I was alive— that was a welcome relief. However, my descriptive words for myself are visionary, coach, detailed, real, innovative, learner, and fun. As I compared the two sets of descriptions, there was some overlap, but not everything matched. I would say anal and detailed go together (hers is the slang version), alive and fun, intelligent and learner, authentic and real. Bless her heart, she has heard me say countless of times during her young years, "You must be intentional" "Be intentional, young lady." "Do things with intention." Consequently, I was tickled when I saw that was how she described me. I am happy to know that at least she is listening to her mother!

When you look at a few of my descriptors, in fairness, they are primarily career-focused, so it is not surprising that my daughter sees me from a child's perspective and as her mom. Whereas my co-workers would never describe me as fabulous or perhaps important; likewise, my daughter would not necessarily see me as innovative or even understand how to assign that description to the role I play in her life. I had a similar experience with my husband. There was enough overlap to conclude that my brand with my family is relatively strong and matches how I want to be viewed and perceived today.

After doing this personal brand assessment for many years, I realize that I still have room for improvement. The main takeaway is that your personal brand can and will evolve. Who you are and how you want to be perceived today may change over time, and you can evolve this because it is not a one and done. Personal branding is a continuous process. Your priorities in life may change, and your position in life may change, so be comfortable knowing that personal branding is an iterative process. You shall forever remain in constant motion managing your brand *signature,* yet you can reap the benefits and rewards along the journey.

Developing your brand means that you are sharing your story with others. It is very important that others feel as though they know you. It's about deepening relationships and your network to be present and prepared as you find opportunities (or as opportunities find you). When you are in sync with your brand, you can attract others and build relationships beyond the superficial. Keep in mind, you are always being evaluated and interviewed for roles and jobs that may or may not exist yet. Personally, professionally, the way you talk, play, work, and interact all count. All these things—even status—happens because people think they know who you are and believe you fit in with them. Think about relationships and your loyalty to brands. We buy from people and brands we trust. It's no different, as I said before: if they believe you fit in, they hire you, nominate you, sponsor you, promote you and so on because they think they know your story.

> " **Developing your brand means that you are sharing your story with others.** "

What is Your Story?

A story has three primary elements. It should be attention-grabbing; relevant and memorable; and have a beginning, middle, and end. The story we want to tell is not an autobiography, yet it is a way to help others understand who you are, your value to them, what audience you serve, and how you stand out. In the next chapter, we will explore the brand discovery process to begin crafting your brand *signature* and statement. For now, I want to introduce you to a few key attributes that may help you create your story.

- **Passion**

  As I shared in Chapter One, passion will keep you going when the going gets tough! Those words, spoken by the famous magician David Copperfield, have never been truer. Your passions energize you and make you attractive to others.

  What lights your fire?

  _____

  _____

  _____

- **Superpowers**

  I love this descriptor; it makes me feel strong. Some of us discount our strengths because we deliver these skills with little to no effort. However, what is obvious or easy to you can be amazing to others.

  What do you do better than others?

  _____

  _____

  _____

- **Values**

  Your values are your operating principles. They impact how you feel, behave, and react. The first step in aligning yourself with your values is knowing what they are and what gets in the way of your ability to live in full alignment with them.

  What are your values?

  _____

  _____

  _____

- **Purpose**

  This is the topic that gives me chills. Your purpose is how you want to contribute to the world. I enjoy operating in realms that are greater than myself. That is perhaps why I have stayed in healthcare for so long, doing work that empowers others to live healthier, more active lives. I understand that mission is much bigger than me. I also experience gratification from my personal branding work. It is about helping clients go from reputation to reward and achieve joy and success by unleashing their power through personal branding. I could go on and on. Just remember, your purpose does not have to be one-dimensional; it can encompass several things.

What is your biggest hope or dream?

_____

_____

_____

- **Differentiation**

  We have touched on this one already. How do you stand out? If what you offer is the same as everyone else, you are a commodity, not an irreplaceable brand. Understand and live your differentiation so you can attract the attention of those making decisions about you.

  What sets you apart from your peers?

  _____

  _____

  _____

These story elements and personal attributes, along with your descriptor words, will help you develop your brand *signature* and story to present to others Now, let's get started.

Chapter Six

Who Are You?

Thus far, we have covered some essential information on personal branding, and I trust you are eager to begin the brand discovery process. The brand discovery process is the process of figuring out what you want to represent today and in the future. It is time for action, so have your descriptor words and attributes handy.

We will start by creating a brand statement. A brand statement is distinctly yours and yours alone. It sums up your unique promise of value. It is your million-dollar minute, as my mentor Linda Clemons, so eloquently says. Using your six descriptive words and attributes, along with the story elements, create a statement consisting of 1-2 sentences or phrases that answer what you do best (value), who you serve (audience), and how you do it uniquely. Keep in mind that this will evolve as you do, so don't get discouraged.

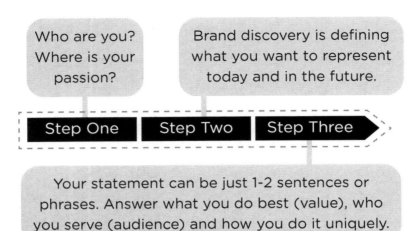

Who are you? Where is your passion?

Brand discovery is defining what you want to represent today and in the future.

Step One   Step Two   Step Three

Your statement can be just 1-2 sentences or phrases. Answer what you do best (value), who you serve (audience) and how you do it uniquely.

In my experience, people really have a hard time talking about themselves; it's not very natural unless you are narcissistic. We love to share the accomplishments and skills of others while often overshadowing our own. Besides, why would anyone think we were anything short of boring, right? Wrong. I think back to that day in 2009 when I choked. It was not natural or comfortable for me to talk about myself to the CEO I was meeting for the first time. I did not know what was appropriate to share, and I certainly did not want to seem full of myself, as I desperately wanted to make a good impression. Well, we know how that turned out for me, but if given the opportunity today, I know exactly what I would say. I shared before that the things we do effortlessly that seem like no big deal to us, may be amazing to others. Do not shortchange your gifts and talents, the world needs all of you!

Creating a brand statement is a critical step in developing your personal brand; if you do not share who you are and advocate for yourself, who do you think is going to do it for you? You never know when you will be stuck in the elevator or encounter a very important person that can change your life. Your personal brand statement is similar to an elevator speech; however, it should not contain your job title or job description. You are much more than a title, and as we know, titles come and go. It is strictly about YOU. With a powerful and interesting branding statement, you should be capable of sharing valuable information about yourself in 30 seconds or less. Remember, the goal is to grab someone's attention with your statement and leave them wanting more. Now, take a moment to create your unique brand statement.

Here are a few examples: These concepts almost jump off the page with energy and a clear value proposition.

> *Master organizer with an eye for detail, meticulously creates and executes special events. "You name it, and I will plan it with confidence and enthusiasm."*

> *Dynamic speaker, author, and coach with a passion for helping corporate professionals and entrepreneurs achieve joy and success by unleashing the power of personal branding. "I help others live authentically, articulate their value, and differentiate themselves to earn more, lead more, and win more."*

This example is specific to a department or team:

> *Specialized marketers within the multi-channel engagement team who collaborate with brand teams and other functions to provide expertise in non-personal healthcare provider channels and platforms, including current and emerging digital technologies.*

Now, that wasn't so bad, was it? Keep working at it, and before you know it, the words will roll off your tongue. You can then add the "how you do it" when

" Your actions must match your words. "

the person shows interest in learning more. I am constantly asked; how do you make your brand statement believable and not hokey sounding? The answer is simple: Your Actions. Your actions must match your words. If you are claiming that you are an expert, be an exceptional expert at something that provides real value. It comes down to the experience you can provide others. Remember, this is an iterative process that should evolve as you grow and reprioritize what is important in your life. With a solid personal branding statement, you are well on your way to developing your brand.

———— **Chapter Seven** ————

Maximizing Your Personal Brand

Congratulations! Can I tell you how proud I am of the work you have done thus far to create your brand *signature*? You are unleashing the power of personal branding and can begin to reap the benefits of going from reputation to reward to earn more, lead more, and win more. I recognize it is hard work and not for the faint of heart, but truly, if it was easy, everyone would be doing it, and your personal brand would no longer make you distinctive. So, kudos for sticking with it.

Take a moment to visualize the power and influence you will soon enjoy. What will you do to stand out, attract clients, or get that promotion you have been wanting? How about the joy of living authentically and helping others with your expertise? People will start recognizing your expertise and seek you out because you will be sharing and engaging on social media, at work, and in other settings. There will be no secret as to what you do well—your superpower.

Then, visualize success because you are and will continue to achieve your aim and purpose. You will soon be enjoying the new fruits of your powerful brand *signature*, and the satisfaction and gratification in serving others will be rewarded in ways unimaginable. You, my friend, are leveling up, reaching for new heights.

In this chapter, the work toward managing and maximizing your brand begins. As I have shared many times throughout this book, this is not a one-time event. Personal branding is a continuous process that will evolve with you. Managing your personal brand is much like managing your stock portfolio. You must continuously decide how to make your personal brand more valuable by knowing what skill sets, capabilities, and resources to invest in and which not to throughout the course of your career.

This can also be called managing your leadership image. As you may recall, I shared with you that you are the leader of YOU, and it is your job to manage your identity to have the most impactful value and significance to others. Whether you own your business or work for a company, you must think like an entrepreneur who is constantly in search of their leadership impact and influence. Unfortunately, most individuals do not know how or cease to manage their personal brand. Thus, they lose career momentum, focus, and impact along the way. Often, when this happens, they have lost the intentionality of managing their brand.

You must dedicate time and strategically contemplate and develop your next steps and remain engaged. Make sure you are not allowing limiting beliefs to creep back into your thoughts. Remain positive and know that if you fall off the wagon, you will just get back up and pick up where you left off. Once you get the hang of it, managing your brand will become a lifestyle like diet and exercise.

If you are strategically leading in ways that come naturally to you and making decisions before circumstances force your hand, you are allowing your personal brand to evolve and flourish. This means that you are proactively managing your brand rather than allowing those around you to define who you are and what you stand for. Continue to stay in control of your narrative.

As the workplace of the future continues to be more about boundaryless environments, the importance of your job title will diminish, and your personal brand will become the ultimate identifier of what you are able to deliver and how you can contribute to the growth of your business or organization. In managing your personal brand, it is important to trust yourself and value your distinction. This means that you should become comfortable as a leader and influencer and with sharing your knowledge and wisdom. It's about you allowing those around you to experience the real you, not your title.

Glen Llopis , best-selling author and entrepreneur wrote that the ebbs and flows of your career require you to make important choices about how to give your personal brand value; equally, you must be aware of how your personal brand translates into and delivers tangible and measurable ROI to those you serve. Every day, every week, every month, you must be mindful of how your personal brand can elevate your relevancy, impact, and influence—and it's your responsibility to define its distinction before someone else does.

Part of that distinction includes your everyday interactions, the way you talk, work, and play. I know this probably goes without saying, yet I appeal to a broad audience and feel it is worth the mention. Always maintain a positive and professional appearance in keeping with your brand. Managing your personal brand requires you to be a great role model, mentor, and/or voice that others can depend on. Successful personal brands earn and build credibility, and credibility starts by articulating the values unique to you and then demonstrating that you walk the talk, so make sure your actions mirror your words. At the end of the day, it's not about tools, it's about people and your value to them. Think of it this way: if you have no traffic, you don't need roads. Bring value to those you serve.

Be responsible and accountable to your brand. Personal branding is the ultimate individual responsibility. That is why it is called "personal branding." No one should manage your personal brand but you. Yes, others can influence it (e.g., mentors, sponsors, advisors), yet in the end, you must make the commitment to manage it.

Be consistent. Once you have developed your story and your brand, be consistent in how you represent yourself to others. You are building influence and gaining the trust of others. When others

> **" When branding, avoid confusion at all costs. Confused people don't buy. "**

know what to expect from you, they become comfortable, feel they know you and that you belong, and then and only then will they open doors and create opportunities for you. If you are sending mixed messages and you show up one way online and another offline, you create confusion. When branding, avoid confusion at all costs. Confused people don't buy. Period!

I purposely saved this section for the end of this chapter because now I need to have a heart-to-heart with you. It's time for some "Real Talk" from your "Brandthrupist", after all, we're friends now. That's what close associates and friends call me: the "Brandthrupist" of personal branding because I give the gift of authenticity as I help others achieve joy and success through the power of branding.

Ok, here goes. Carefully select your resources and align your brand. What does this mean? Let me say it in a few different ways. "All money isn't good money," and you must be mindful of who you choose to engage for business purposes, also "If you want to kill a big dream, tell it to small-minded people." Not everyone will understand and align with your vision.

They won't like the key changes you are making in your life to achieve a powerful brand *signature*. They will not appreciate that you are no longer available to them. It's ok. Remember, it is not for everyone's understanding and that is why it is important that you evaluate your resources and your tribe. You need to surround yourself with like-minded individuals. As my mentor, Linda Clemons—global sales trainer, body language expert and CEO of Sisterprenuer, Inc.—says, "If all your friends are broke, you are likely going to be broke. If you are the smartest one in the room, who is pouring into you?"

I cannot emphasize this enough, and I have witnessed, firsthand, personal brands either implode or never gain momentum because of the company a person keeps or does business with. Make sure your friends and business partners are respected, credible, trustworthy individuals. If you are afraid of what someone may say or how someone may act in social and professional settings, they don't belong in your inner circle. People automatically assume that "birds of a feather flock together." If John has a reputation as a shyster businessman and you are always seen with John, guess what? Odds are that they have that same impression of you. I am not saying it is fair, or right for that matter, but it is what it is, and we all have biases—good, bad, or indifferent.

Please don't shoot the messenger. I'm just keeping it real. I know, we all have friends from way back that have stayed in our lives despite our paths going in different directions. I am not saying you should throw them out with the bathwater. I am simply saying that there is a time and place for everything. Don't bring excess baggage to the table when you are trying to level up. People need to bring more than their appetites because you, too, need to be fed. You need supportive, encouraging people who will be honest with you, challenge you, and push you beyond your limits.

Chapter Eight

Common Mistakes When Building a Personal Brand Signature

In anything we strive to achieve, there are often barriers, pitfalls, and mistakes along the way. I will share with you some common mistakes to avoid when creating and managing your personal brand *signature*. Some branding practices will happen through trial and error—it is only natural—yet common mistakes can be avoided if you are aware of the pitfalls. There are a lot of opinions when it comes to the most common mistakes, along with a plethora of commentaries on what to avoid including focusing too much on themselves, not sharing the right content, focusing on the career they have versus the one they want, and so on.

Here are a few of the more common personal branding mistakes proposed by me and branding strategist Ryan Erskine.

1. **Thinking personal branding does not pertain to you.**

   Whether you're an entrepreneur, a C-suite executive, or somewhere in between, personal branding has a place in helping you take your business or career to the next level. It is all about marketing your value and distinguishing yourself to take control of your story and turn your reputation into reward.

   Whatever path you're on, your online and offline presence can either help you or hurt you along the way. Don't make the mistake of thinking personal branding doesn't pertain to you. We are all a brand!

2. **Pretending to be someone you're not.**

   When we're first dating someone new, we often try to show the best side of ourselves. Our apartments may look a little neater than usual, or perhaps our jobs suddenly become more interesting and impressive than they were a week ago.

   In small amounts, this practice can help you gain someone's attention and forge a deeper connection. However, if you take this too far, you risk becoming someone you're not for the sake of continuing a relationship. Remember, the joy of creating a positive brand *signature* is that you can be yourself, your true authentic self.

Don't get caught up in trying to impress people and lose the essence of who you are and what you truly want to be known for. If you do, you risk having your strategy backfire. Nobody wants to date, hire, or do business with a fraud. Authenticity is key, both for relationships and personal brands. Don't make the mistake of pretending to be someone you're not.

3. Waiting until something bad happens.

Dentists recommend brushing your teeth twice a day, every day. Can you imagine what would happen if you only brushed your teeth once they started turning brown and rotting? You'd probably get gum disease, have some brutal toothaches, and your smile would leave a lot to be desired. Once you get to this point, it's usually too late to fix everything. At the very least, there would be a lot of ground to make up. Brushing your teeth on an ongoing basis is a far more effective way to maintain a winning smile and maintain oral hygiene.

Personal branding works in much the same way. It's harder to take control of your online narrative once there is already something bad that you need to contend with. Many people only realize how important their brand *signature* is once they have a problem. But that's a classic mistake. Personal branding can be more effective, and less of a headache, when it's done preventatively. A little work now can make things a lot easier later.

4. **Ignoring others in the brand discovery process.**

When creating a personal brand, you cannot overestimate the importance of external consulting from friends, family, coworkers, or a professional branding firm. You are not creating a brand to impress yourself; you are creating a brand to impress and attract others, not to mention that it is very difficult to see yourself from others' perspectives. Talking your brand out with someone else can help you get a little distance from the narrative you already hold in your own head.

The consequences of making branding mistakes are scary and can cost you the reward and joy you are seeking. You can run with what you believe to be a "great idea," only to find out afterward it didn't resonate with a core group of your target audience. The lesson here is that a little outside perspective goes a long way.

5. **Underestimating the time required to develop a great brand.**

Building and maintaining an effective personal brand consists of a lot more than just having a website and a few social media channels. It's about providing people with real value again and again. It's about distinguishing yourself from your competition and making yourself memorable to the people you want to engage and interact with the most.

That's no easy feat, especially in a noisy digital world. It takes five to seven impressions for someone to remember a brand on average, so imagine the work you need to put in to get in front of the right people repeatedly. One of the most efficient ways to do this is through influencers. They might be colleagues and family members in your existing network, your friends from way back when, or complete strangers in your industry who would be happy to collaborate. Do yourself a favor and find these influencers first so you can get the traffic and engagement you desire. If you are not willing to do the work to get yourself seen by the people who matter, then you won't get the reach and reward you desire. Be patient, consistent and stay in action.

6. **Creating brand confusion.**

A confused mind doesn't buy! I've heard this saying for years, and it is so true. As a buyer, if you are not sure what you are getting, do not understand the outcome you will achieve, do not know what the product or service will offer, or do not have a clear understanding of the brand delivering it, you are highly unlikely to make a purchase decision.

Therefore, you should avoid the pitfall of creating confusion with your personal brand. This often happens when the person you represent online does not match who you are offline, or when there is no clarity and consistency in your brand. Who you represent in action must mirror the brand *signature* you created with your words, your story, and brand statement. Do not send mixed messages to your audience. Be clear, concise, strategic, and intentional and live your personal brand *signature* in a manner that takes you from reputation to reward. Clarity breeds support and if you attract the right people with the right message at the right time, true engagement can take place, and you will earn more, lead more, and win more.

7. **Trying to appeal to everyone.**

One of the most common mistakes is attempting to appeal to everyone by being too broad and not targeting a niche market. I will be the first to say it is very difficult when you believe you have a product or service with broad appeal. While you may expand your reach over time, you must first identify your niche market so you can tailor your products, services, and marketing strategies to reach your intended audience.

I struggled with this, as I believe my target audience consist of entrepreneurs/business owners and corporate professionals. When I completed my market segmentation, I realized that while my information can remain the same for the entrepreneurs and corporate professionals, how I market to them is not the same. What an entrepreneur is trying to accomplish is in stark contrast to what a corporate professional wants to achieve. An entrepreneur is looking for influence, network and attracting clients, whereas a corporate professional may be looking to advance their career, get promoted, and feel valued.

Again, this is where patience comes into play. Start with one target so that your marketing strategy can be laser focused. Then, once you have a handle on that niche market, you can expand your reach.

8. Thinking that personal and professional brands are separate.

One key mistake that people make is thinking their personal brand and professional brand are two different things. They should absolutely be the same and you need only one brand. You want to be the same authentic person at home, with friends, at work, and at play. While your interests and actions may vary in different settings, who you are and your value to others does not change. There is no reason to create multiple brands that will create confusion. Your brand *signature* is about you and only you. It should encompass who you are personally and professionally.

I had a recent experience while conducting market research with an individual for a personal branding online course I was creating. She was a resume writer and was adamant that she was tired of her clients working with personal branding experts and consultants. I didn't understand why she would be upset, considering those clients should come to her with clarity and focus, which would make her job easy. Yet, she said she would never hire someone for personal branding and people don't need personal branding; they need professional branding because a personal brand does not get them a job. Once I realized she was making a clear distinction between two perceived brands, I attempted to help her understand the misperception and explained that they should not be separate; they are the same.

Oh boy, she did not like that, and not only did she not agree with me, she was no longer interested in taking part in my market research project. I completely understand how it can appear confusing when you consider your personal versus professional interest and I empathize when others do not understand the difference, yet please do not make the mistake of thinking you need more than one brand. The core of who you are should be intertwined in everything you do and how you represent yourself.

9. **Failing to manage your brand *signature*.**

You put all the work and effort into thinking about who you are, working through the brand discovery process, and creating your personal brand *signature* and story to share with your target audience. You have created a few social media profiles and perhaps a webpage. Congratulations. But then you do nothing else and expect results. This a common mistake that often causes people to lose momentum and personal brands to fail.

I cannot stress enough that you must stay in action and be consistent in engaging with your audience—don't just make connections; build meaningful relationships. Individuals who are like-minded and have similar interests make great partners. Look for people who serve the same audience but who offer services that complement yours rather than compete with yours. You can partner with these types of individuals and bring value to one another while achieving your individual goals.

Do not try to build relationships before giving to your audience. Make sure you empathize and express an understanding of your audience's needs before you ask them for something. You must stay in action and evolve your brand, not only through relationships, but by enhancing your skills and value to others. Maintaining your brand *signature* takes effort, and you must stay in control of the reputation and image that others see.

10. Choosing quantity over quality.

Getting followers for the sake of growing your follower count is a rookie mistake. Believe me: I have made this mistake on several platforms. To this day, I am baffled as to why people want to connect for the sake of it. I learned early that if people are not engaged, they do not necessarily want to connect with you personally. They are merely boosting numbers. If you ask them for something, you often get crickets. Perhaps most of us can find pleasure in the number of connections as we look at the large numbers of likes and followers we have. However, if you have 200,000 followers but get no engagement on your content, what's the point? You are being ignored, and nobody new is thinking about your business. You're not fooling anyone.

What is more valuable to you? 200,000 uninterested followers or two dozen diehard fans that engage with your content every week? I'll go with the engaged followers every time. They're much more likely to tell their friends and share your content—and to buy from you. If you are interested in growing a following with your intended audience, there are tools out there, such as Crowdfire, Hootsuite, and Simplifi Me (to name a few) to assist you based on keywords, hashtags, and specific targets.

────────── **Chapter Nine** ──────────

Conclusion

Personal branding is one of the single most important things you can do to ensure you are the author of your story. Your personal brand *signature* is a unique extension of who you are and maintaining a strong personal brand will help build credibility and trust to convert reputation to reward to achieve a life of joy and success. Live authentically as you articulate and demonstrate your value to others, it will bring you the greatest satisfaction and allow you to differentiate and stand-out. Constantly be in search of improving your skills and reputation so you are ready when the next opportunity arises.

You are the CEO of your personal brand, if you do not take ownership, someone else will. A positive brand *signature* will allow you to earn more, lead more and win more. Your reputation can be monetized in a positive and strategic way. Be intentional in knowing that your brand *signature* should evolve as you do, so don't get hung up on perfection, instead be in constant action. As you take the journey, rewards will come along the way, take great care in cultivating and maximizing your power and influence so it works for good and not evil.

Create a brand that is simple and will stay in the minds of others while building a consistent impression of your own quality. Practice, practice, practice your story. When the CEO of your company ask you to tell them about yourself, you will be confident and prepared.

Relationships matter and when people believe they know you and you fit in they will support you in many ways including sponsorship, promotions, nominations, and they will marry you and loan you money. Never underestimate the value your brand *signature* affords you. Know your audience. You can have vast networks, email contacts, clients and advocates to help you promote yourself or your business, but remember, "People Don't Care How Much You Know, Until They Know How Much You Care".

Maximize social media to develop influence and create a positive digital footprint. Strive to be a great role model, mentor and voice that others can depend upon. To create the reputation that leads to rewards, you must walk the talk and ensure your online and offline reputation match. People are watching, even when you do not think they are. It's all about negotiations and you are consistently being sized up. You are now equipped to unleash the power of your personal brand!

Chapter Ten

The Power of Social Media

Working in the marketing department of a pharmaceutical company afforded me the opportunity to appreciate the evolution of technology. I remember working, back in my sales days when paper maps were used to find our customer locations (you can barely find a paper map nowadays). I would carry a notebook and printed customer list for account management, manual call logs, and I used snail mail.

And then came the days of Blackberry's and Palm Pilots. By 2003, the world was very different after the introduction of social media. By the time I moved to the marketing organization in 2008, technology had advanced drastically with the internet, email, and websites considered everyday necessities. Everyone used Google as a method to search for information, and mobilization and app development were being hailed as sexy new technologies. There is so much more today that is designed to keep us constantly connected. We've come a long way, baby!

The internet, digital technology, and social media have taken the world by storm. Some suggest it is a cluttered environment. However, I would say it's a ripe opportunity for you to market your brand *signature*. We have the ability to access people, businesses, and information with the strike of a key and the click of a button. We are all connected, and connectivity allows you to create networks, build credibility, and drive profits from your living rooms and offices.

This is not a fad, trend, or fluke. This is our way of life. So, if you are not connected to social media, this is my challenge to you: Start now! Gaining followers, getting likes, making connections, influencing others and propelling your brand further faster are just a mobile phone, tablet, or laptop click away.

You're a brand. I'm a brand. We're all brands, whether we choose to be or not. The key is to create the best personal brand we can by utilizing the tools at our disposal. A strong social media presence is perhaps the greatest gift you can give yourself and your business. Make connections where the audience is, don't just focus on channels; they change. Individuals with successful personal brands take control to ensure that who they are online matches who they are in person.

The goal is to create a positive digital footprint by ensuring that your social interactions are aligned with your brand image. That means you need to use social media responsibly. I will not elaborate on this other than by saying that once you put it out there, you cannot take it back. Social media is a lot like words, think before you engage/speak. Remember one of the benefits of personal branding is having power and influence to achieve the joy and success you desire. If done correctly, you can enjoy a steady stream of clients, rewarding partnerships and sponsors, greater mindshare, associations with top-notch leaders, and much more.

Kevan Lee, VP of marketing at Buffer, created a list of five steps to building your personal brand on social media. Inspired by some great thought leaders on the topic, he put together five personal branding tips, and several of these have helped me in my quest to optimize my social brand. Here is my take on his five steps.

1. **Choose your expertise.**

   We have already discussed this, so you should be good here. The key is making sure you are focused and that your expertise is specific and niche, as this will give you more opportunities to build credibility and prove that you know what you are talking about. You can target key audiences and provide content that is relevant. Keep in mind that there are lots of entrepreneurs competing for online attention. If content is the fuel for your personal brand, social media is the engine.

2. Keep the same name, profile, pic, imagery, and look across your social profiles.

Keeping a consistent profile helps others find you easily, and it helps cement a picture of you in the minds of others. The fewer variations you have (ideally, you'll create one consistent look), the more likely it is to be memorable. In a perfect world, you'd have the same username in every location. If this isn't possible for you, come up with a standard variation to use when your first choice is already taken.

I learned this the hard way, for more than a decade, I was known as Yolanda Johnson-Moton and had a strong following and digital footprint. Deciding to take my current husband's name professionally meant I had to start creating my online presence pretty much from scratch when it couldn't be cross-referenced. However, recognizing that this was one of those arguments I would never win (I tried the "I do love you, but honey, I have a strong professional following" line but to no avail), I bit the bullet all in the name of love, and Yolanda M. Smith it is!

3. Post every day to your most valued social profiles.

How will others get to know you and your brand? Making yourself easy to find is the first step toward having a great brand. The next step is sharing your enthusiasm and expertise with others. Taking an active role on your social channels is key to gaining influence and followers. You may be asking how many channels you should take part in. My suggestion is that if you are just starting to engage with social media, you should pick two platforms: one high-engagement platform and one high-value platform.

High-engagement platforms include platforms like Twitter and Instagram, and high-value ones are "long" platforms like Facebook, YouTube, LinkedIn, and blogging/podcasting sites where you can create content. Understand the functional and emotional needs of your audience and find out where they engage.

4. **Join a chat, group, or community to reach out to others.**

Sharing consistently on social media will help you draw others to you and your brand. Along with this, you can take a proactive approach to social media engagement by getting involved with your community. Here are a few tips from Barry Feldman on getting connected.

- Follow up with new connections you make promptly, stay in touch, and always follow through on your promises.

- Connect the people in your network to each other.

- Surround yourself with top-notch people.

- Don't let awe stop you. Have the confidence to reach out to the best.

- Study the networks of successful friends and leaders in your niche and follow their lead.

- Ask your connections if there's anything you can do for them.

- Tell people you're excited to hear their stories. They'll be glad to share them.

- Make yourself available to your peers and organizations.

5. **Monitor mentions of your name and reply quickly.**

A good rule of thumb is to respond to mentions within 24 hours. I try to be very responsive, though I have a very busy life outside of managing my brand. If you are on multiple channels, trying to stay engaged with all of them may seem overwhelming. It is perfectly ok to start slow, recognizing this is not a sprint but a marathon and you are in it for the long haul. With that said, if you are mentioned by others, make an effort to acknowledge them.

Following these tips for building a personal brand through social media can help you strategize how to present yourself online. Social branding is useful for everyone, not just the big names. One of the most overlooked aspects of social business and social media is the power of the brand signature. Unfortunately, many professionals wrongly assume that personal branding is only for those looking to be "famous" or become some type of online or social marketing "guru." This couldn't be further from the truth. Establishing a personal brand on social media is something everyone should do and can lead to great rewards. I'm counting on you—connect with me on social media.

linkedin.com/in/branding4success
Twitter: @_YolandaSmith
Facebook: fb.me/branding4success
Website: yolanda-smith.com

Chapter Eleven

Managing Through a Brand Crisis

Never Say Never. I learned this the hard way. I thought that my reputation and image were bulletproof. Oh, boy, I was about to be in for a huge surprise. The company I worked for was going through a lot of organizational changes, and you know how it is when faced with change: you can either go with the flow, buck the system, or be a slow adopter who eventually comes along. In this case, the leaders knew that things needed to change operationally. We were top-heavy, and operating expenses were out of the normal range, so essentially, we were outliers for our industry. It was common knowledge that we needed to reign things in. After much discussion and opportunities for improvement, the company decided to offer a voluntary retirement package to all eligible employees after they had undergone, less than a year earlier, a restructuring. My department was shuffled around, and within a years' time, I had gone through two bosses, and by the end of the early retirement offering period, both were gone, and I was working on my third. This was extremely unsettling and disruptive. Yet as a leader, I had to keep a strong front for my team. That meant I had to encourage and motivate them to remain focused on the current job at hand while being transparent regarding what was happening, with the assurance that we would get through this tough time.

Then came my new boss. I have said and will continue to say that a company is only as good as its leaders, and while I have heard horror stories of bad leaders in the past, I can honestly say, I had yet to live it and be a part of that cast of characters. My boss was announced and reported to their new role with little to no expertise in our industry. They had healthcare credentials but no experience leading a high-performing, high-functioning team. This was their third role in a year-and-a-half at the company, signaling a red flag to all. Nonetheless, it became quickly apparent that they had no intention of sitting idle. They were determined to make their mark.

Well, I became the target, and for whatever reason, their mission was to seek and destroy. I have never served in the military, but I understand once you lock in on your target, your job is to attack with full force until the job is accomplished. Welcome to WWMe. I was under attack. I was in a crisis!

Prior to being under this new boss's leadership, I had experienced a wonderful career at this organization, innovating and transforming our industry relations in ways that had not been attempted before. I received the most prestigious award at the organization just the year prior while also being named a "Woman of Influence" by one of the most reputable business news organizations in our city. I did not take this lightly because, out of all the remarkable women in the city, I was honored among a chosen few. Yet, within months of receiving this honor, I was being challenged, and my credibility being questioned because this person, who didn't even know me, simply did not like me. More importantly, they did not feel I deserved the recognition that my reputation was garnering.

In their quest to destroy me, I was spoken to condescendingly, treated like a first-time manager (and sometimes like a child), even though I had over a decade of successful leadership and even more professional experience. Everything I had created, the team I built, and all our accomplishments came under scrutiny. It was as if my boss was on a witch hunt to find something, anything to prove that I was unworthy of the position, the accolades, promotions, and recognition that had been bestowed upon me. I was told I could no longer facilitate my masterclasses on personal branding, a course which was consistently full and one of a few opportunities for personal employee development. To add insult to injury, I was scheduled to keynote at our annual speaker series and was told I could no longer participate, with no reasonable justification.

I was horrified, humiliated and hurt. The posters were hung along all corridors and the event was being actively promoted, yet I knew I would not be taking the stage. People were confused and felt like I was letting them down, and it did not look good for my credibility and professional image, my personal brand came into question and it was all beyond me and what I was prepared to handle. It happened swiftly and I did not believe in a million light-years, this would have been the outcome. This person was creating the narrative and running plays while I was not in the room to defend myself. Moreover, to my detriment, I was not in control of my own personal brand. Again, I honestly did not react as I was unaware of what was happening behind the scenes. What I did know is that my boss was relentless. Because it happened so fast, I felt as though I had been hit by a ton of bricks simply because it was surreal, unimaginable and unconscionable. How could the company allow this to happen?

This was a tough period mentally, spiritually, and financially. You are probably wondering what I did. I submit to you that, while I am far from a perfect person, I did nothing wrong that would warrant this level of treatment. I still scratch my head from time to time, and the only thing I can conclude is that I did not appease this boss, and I likely neglected to give them the power and authority over me that they desired, whether it was deserved or not. This is not the power I spoke about that comes with your brand *signature*. This is the other kind of power—control of others—and yet this was all new to me. I had never been managed at this level in my career, not even as a newbie. I was accustomed to leadership, autonomy and support. So, while I was taken aback by their leadership style (or lack thereof), I perhaps was being a bit protective of my territory and what I felt belonged to me. After all, I had started the department from the ground up.

When I think about my emotional intelligence during this time, I realize that I may not have handled this invasion very well, and I probably went on the defensive. I'm being genuine—this is me being authentic and sharing with you that I became very protective and nurturing of my team. This sergeant was going to protect her troops. As an aside, I believe I may have become too comfortable in my role, which is another lesson: Be careful not to get too comfortable with your position or status. It can be taken away quickly. A strong personal brand, however, can weather any storm.

During this time, my boss had what I did not: a sponsor and supportive leader who gave them complete autonomy to do as they pleased, in part based on their mutual credentials, not skill. The lesson here is that you cannot assume that because a person is accomplished in one area that they will automatically perform well in others. (The system failed them also.)

My boss proved to be unrelenting, even baffling others who were witnessing or who were a part of this mayhem. No one could understand their motive. In the end, my entire department was dissolved, and the reasons given were difficult to challenge, limited resources and budget cuts. In my opinion, they were not successful at destroying me, so they took down the entire department to prove their point and be viewed as right. In war, sometimes there are innocent casualties. My team were the casualties in this case. No one deserved this.

I will leave you with another nugget and then it's on to how to manage in a crisis. I heard this saying years ago, and I don't know who to credit, but it has stuck with me and been my position and a mainstay in my coaching and mentoring: "Influential people are not concerned with always being right, they are concerned with being effective." It is more important to get people to do what you need them to do versus spending energy on proving you are always right.

I tell you this story to share that I never thought it would happen to me, and it did. I had to dig deep and put into practice the things I had been teaching for years. If I had recognized what was happening earlier, I believe it would have yielded a very different result. Again, in full transparency (we're friends, right?), I had become comfortable in my position. It is important to be prepared for a brand crisis in which your credibility, authenticity, and overall brand *signature* are tested, because not everyone will like you or wish you well. I survived and found another role, though that was not the case for all my team—there were definitely casualties among us. It was a sad time but a great lesson in character and strength.

I held my head high. people were shocked that I stayed with the organization, but I was not going to allow my boss to win, and I was still standing. And once the dust settled, those who knew me, and my brand remained on team Yolanda and respected me even more. Those who didn't, well, I am not sure what they think, but one thing is for sure: they know I possess resilience and strength and that if you come for me, you best bring the entire army. As for that leader, let's just say it did not bode well for them, either. Weeks after I secured another position, they were removed from their leadership role and became an individual contributor. I wish them well.

In the words of Warren Buffett, "It takes 20 years to build a reputation and five minutes to ruin it. If you think about that, you'll do things differently." It's not a matter of if but a matter of when you'll be faced with a crisis. Did you know that most executives use personal branding for online reputation management, or they have someone doing it for them and here's why.

- Reputation damage is the No. 1 risk concern for business executives around the world, and 88 percent say they are explicitly focusing on reputation risk as a key business challenge.

- Of all executives, 87 percent rate reputation risk as more important or much more important than other strategic risks their companies are facing.

- Of respondents who experienced a reputation risk event, 41 percent say loss of revenue was the biggest impact. I can certainly attest to this as one who experienced a significant impact financially when experiencing a personal brand crisis.

Reputation has always been a big deal for companies, but now we as individuals must contend with it both offline and online. With reputation damage as the No. 1 risk companies face today, it's no wonder executives are preventatively investing in online reputation management as an insurance measure. And with the social media movement, you must be careful to maintain a positive appearance, as it is much easier to get sucked into social drama, as I call it. When faced with a personal branding crisis, don't be quick to react, it is important to take pause and understand that the secret of crisis management is not good versus bad, it is preventing the bad from getting worse.

It is important to have a strategy before a crisis occurs— remember, one of the most important aspects of building any personal brand is to be authentic and genuine. If you have a strategy, you can be prepared. When faced with a situation where your reputation is being questions, take time to evaluate your current brand and identify blind spots and behaviors that may have created the negative perception. Focus on the target audience and try to understand their needs, what they believe to be true about you, and what perceptions you have created, whether intentional or not. Be accountable.

Once you have taken the time to assess the situation and understand why a person feels the way they do, then—and only if necessary—do you provide a well-thought-out response. Sometimes silence is golden, as a response can further fuel the fire. Be thoughtful in your approach, recognizing what is real and what is concocted to get a reaction.

Real talk again: you will have HATERS. We all do, those individuals who are not cheering for you will attempt to sabotage you or attempt to prove to others that you are not as great as you seem. My advice? Ignore them. They are not worthy of a response. For those who have genuine concerns, you may want to take the necessary steps to correct their misperceptions of you, especially if they are influential and have large followings in your area of expertise. That may require offline conversations if the concern started online. Above all, do not allow your personal differences or an argument to play out online when your reputation is at stake. It's simply not worth it.

NOTES

NOTES

NOTES

NOTES

ACKNOWLEDGMENTS

I first would like to acknowledge God, my Lord and Savior for everything I am, because without him, I am nothing. Thank you for my family, friends, the gifts and talents you loaned me, for discernment, and most of all, thank you for your grace and mercy. I know God's grace is sufficient, and I give him all the honor and glory.

To my mom, thank you for life and for being a wonderful, thoughtful, and God-fearing woman. To my dad, who has passed on from this earth, you were the best dad a girl could have. Thanks for making me feel special.

I want to acknowledge my husband Kenton, for the love, support, and encouragement he offers me to do the things I am passionate about doing. Thank you for standing in the gap and accepting me as your perfectly, imperfect wife. I love you dearly.

To my son, Austin, who balances me out and encourages me to slow down, relax, and take care of myself, thank you for your loving spirit and maturity. I also want to thank my daughters, Madison and Victoria, for being my biggest cheerleaders and making me feel like I can conquer anything against all odds. I have been blessed with many children that I may not have birthed, but sincerely love just the same: Donald Jr., Brooke, Lil Mason, Quinton, and my goddaughters Kenyada and Raven. I appreciate your love and support. I don't take the "mom" title lightly, and I am honored to have played an instrumental role in your life. I hope that I have enhanced each of you in some small way.

I want to thank my brothers and sister, Archie, Jim, Jason, and Raelynn, from the bottom of my heart. You guys have always been in my corner and have had my back in ways unimaginable. I love you unconditionally. We are family.

To my book coach, Dr. Larthenia Howard, thank you for pushing me to dig deep and make the book better. Your brainstorming sessions helped me to reach beyond the surface to create a book that will truly inspire and help others to create a powerful brand *signature*. We did this!

I wish to acknowledge Linda Clemons, my mentor, for the powerful impact you have had on my life in a short period of time. Your spirit is selfless, yet powerful. You are anointed, and your gifts are plentiful. Thank you for helping me release my fears and for motivating me to keep moving forward to achieve my passion and dreams. I look forward to the places we will go, not to mention, you give the best goodie bags, ever.

To Denola Burton, founder of D.N.A. Publishing, thank you for putting the writing bug in me. I had my book outline on a shelf for several years, and you invited me to be part of an author collaboration that ignited my creativity and motivated me to write my book.

Finally, I would like to thank my crew, you guys know who you are. You have been my rock, my ride-or-die. I am grateful for all the love and support you have given me, through good and bad times. It's rare to have friendships that go back for decades. I am truly fortunate to have many of those, as well as newfound friendships that I have cultivated along the way. Each of you are special in your own way and you keep me honest and true to who I am, challenging me to be the best version of myself. I hope that I have added as much value to you, as you have for me. Thank you for always showing up for me. Friends and family forever. I love you guys.

PROGRAMS AND SERVICES

- **Keynote Speeches**
  - Maximize Your Personal Brand
  - Personal Branding in the Digital Age
  - Branding the Authentic U

- **Masterclass Facilitator**
  - Creating & Maximizing your Personal Brand
  - Creating an Explosive Digital Footprint

- **Corporate Teambuilding**
  - Creating a Team Brand Identity

- **Career Coaching**
  - Group and Individual Sessions

- **Online Course**
  - Reputation to Reward: Creating and Maximizing Your Brand *Signature*

YOLANDA M. SMITH

Yolanda Smith is an expert in the field of Personal Branding. 10+ years of public speaking experience and a passion for helping others achieve their personal best inspired her to found Branding 4 Success, LLC, where she currently serves at chief Brandthrupist, traveling the country; delivering personal branding keynote speeches; and facilitating masterclasses to academic, corporate, and professional organizations. Yolanda helps entrepreneurs and corporate professionals create their brand *signature* to earn more, lead more, and win more.

Yolanda Smith is a parallel-prenuer who also works in the pharmaceutical industry, where she leads the oncology healthcare provider strategy and portfolio for the customer engagement team at Eli Lilly and Company. Prior to this role, Yolanda was the director of external relations. Her team was responsible for strategizing and implementing portfolios and initiatives to educate and enhance Lilly's partnerships with US external stakeholders.

Known for her innovative thinking and ability to implement on her vision, Yolanda's recognition extends broadly. She recently was awarded the 2019 Team Lilly Award for leadership and was selected as one of the *Indianapolis Business Journal's* 2017 "Women of Influence," which recognizes women who have demonstrated professional excellence and leadership through their careers and community service. She earned the prestigious 2017 LRL President's Diversity Award, and in 2016, she was honored with the PM360 ELITE Award for transformational leadership. Yolanda has held various leadership roles in the pharmaceutical industry throughout her career.

Yolanda's educational pursuits earned her a Bachelor of Science degree from Indiana University, Kelley School of Business in marketing and business analysis, and she obtained her MBA with a healthcare concentration from Indiana Wesleyan University.

Yolanda is married with children. She enjoys gardening, is a saltwater aquarium enthusiast, and loves to travel, shop and cook.